THE PHILOSOPHER'S STONED

Compiled by Ann Nelson, alive in Tucson, growing Dahlias. She cannot bear not knowing answers to life's astounding questions. She Kant stand it.

Copyright ©2016
The scanning, uploading and distribution of the contents of this publication via the Internet or via any other means without the permission of the publisher is perfectly okay by me, without prior written permission of both the copyright owner and the author of this book.

INTRODUCTION

If you can improve the silence, keep it funny or interesting. *The Philosopher's Stoned* will prepare you for those magical moments when you find yourself debating the impermanence and illusion of the fundamental truths of our physical dimension.

Altering and enriching consciousness helps to break through illusion and muggled perception. Raised frequencies lift a veil and what is real and true or existential or paradoxical, can be profound. Be ready! Keep this book close, refer to it, roll on it. Meditate on it. Make it a drinking game. It is an adventure in the realms of human knowledge and ancient wisdom. Drink deep. Transform your life through a provocative trip down the proven path of the Philosophers.

This is Earth School. You have exactly NOW to start your soul search to find clarity, wisdom and purposefulness. (Hint: This is a lucid start.)

What is knowledge?
What is the nature of reality?
What is love?
Why can't I make eye contact?

　Philosophy enhances problem-solving capabilities, our understanding, our expression of ideas and our persuasive powers. It can give us foresight, self-knowledge and a sense of direction in life. It confronts the current existential challenges of the world.
　Philosophy explores the deepest, broadest questions of life. Socrates said, "An unexamined life is not worth living." The essence of philosophy is to ask questions, to look beyond the surface and find the substance behind our own convictions. Philosophical reflection lets us escape the unreal world.

　Welcome to the real world. A well-lived life. Enlightened consciousness. An expansion and deepening of the mind. If you are going to be altering your consciousness, beam up to one of the world's oldest subjects of study. Philosophy pursues questions in every dimension of human life.
　Open-mindedness is the single most important characteristic we have as human beings. Free your mind from limiting thoughts. Become inquisitive. Be aware of your judgments and opinions and question where they come from. What is truth?

Open up a whole new realm of possibilities and ideas and be willing to consider or receive new and different ideas while being flexible and adaptive to new experiences. The more you learn the more interesting you become. Wake up and keep waking up more. An open mind is a free mind. Transcend to a higher level of thinking. Go beyond our limited perceptions of reality. Become a life-long learner with a philosophical mind. You won't regret it.

    Bertrand Russell said, "Has the universe any unity of plan or purpose or is it a fortuitous concourse of atoms? Is consciousness a permanent part of the universe, giving hope of indefinite growth in wisdom, or is it a transitory accident on a small planet on which life must ultimately become impossible? Are good and evil of importance to the universe or only to man? Such questions are asked by philosophy, and variously answered by various philosophers."

Philippians 4:8 says, "Finally, brothers and sisters, whatever is true, whatever is noble, whatever is right, whatever is pure, whatever is lovely, whatever is admirable—if anything is **excellent** or praiseworthy – think on these things."

"The Philosopher's Stone" was not a literal substance to turn base metals into gold, but a symbolic process to turn base man into Actualized Self: the process of individuation.

Carl Jung

Listen to the mustn'ts, child.
Listen to the don'ts.
Listen to
The shouldn'ts, the impossibles,
The won'ts. Listen to the never haves, then listen close to me...

Anything can happen, child. Anything can be.

Shel Silverstein

When you realize there is nothing lacking,

the whole world belongs to you.

Lao Tzu

Happiness is not an ideal of reason but of imagination.

Immanuel Kant

If the doors of perception were cleansed everything would appear to man as it is, infinite.

William Blake

Those who don't believe in magic will never find it.

Roald Dahl

There are no physical laws in the universe. They're more like suggestions.

Sri Aurobindo

Be forewarned...applying these teachings may be damaging to your beliefs, disorienting to your mind, and distressing to your ego.

Adyashanti

Science gives us knowledge, but only **philosophy** can give us wisdom.

Will Durant

Whence come I and whither go I? That is the great unfathomable question, the same for every one of us.

Science has no answer to it.

Max Planck

The answer, the strength, the right action or the resource will be there when you need it in the NOW, not before, not after.

Eckhart Tolle

"...don't worry about it kid, okay:

Just tune in;
turn off,
drop out,
drop in,
switch off,
switch on
and explode."

Lennon/McCartney

My advice to people today is as follows: if you take the game of life seriously, if you take your nervous system seriously, if you take your sense organs seriously, if you take the energy process seriously, you must **turn on, tune in and drop out.**

Timothy Leary

*Come writers and critics
Who prophesize with your pen
And keep your eyes wide
The chance won't come again
And don't speak too soon
For the wheel's still in spin
And there's no tellin' who
That it's namin'
For the loser now
Will be later to win
For the times they are a-changin.*

Bob Dylan

to be nobody but yourself in a world which is doing its best to make you everybody else, means to fight the hardest human battle ever and to never stop fighting.

e.e. cummings

A well-adjusted person is one who makes the same mistake twice without getting nervous.

Alexander Hamilton

The knower of the mystery of sound knows the mystery of the whole universe.

Hazrat Inayat Khan

We are powerfully imprisoned by the terms in which we have been conducted to **think.**

Buckminster Fuller

We are an individuated unit of consciousness playing a total immersion virtual reality game wherein our avatars make choices and appear to have physical bodies and live in physical space.

Isaac Asimov

I have believed the best of every man. And find that to believe it is enough to make a bad man show him at his best or even a good man swing his lantern higher.

William Butler Yeats

After silence, that which comes nearest to expressing the inexpressible is music.

Jack Kerouac

Man cannot live without a continuous confidence in something indestructible within himself.

Franz Kafka

Only that in you which is me can hear what I'm saying.

Baba Ram Dass

The past is not dead.

It's not even past.

William Faulkner

All matter originates and exists only by virtue of a force... We must assume behind this force the existence of a conscious and intelligent Mind. This Mind is the matrix of all matter.

Max Planck

It is a mania shared by philosophers of all ages to deny what exists and to explain what does not exist.

Jean-Jacques Rousseau

"I have always loved marijuana. It has been a source of joy and comfort to me for many years. And I still think of it as a basic staple of life, along with beer and ice and grapefruits – and millions of Americans agree with me."

Hunter S. Thompson

"My main hope for myself is to be where I am."

Woody Harrelson

The best time to plant a tree is twenty years ago. The second best time is now.

Chinese Proverb

Wonder is the feeling of the philosopher,
and philosophy begins in wonder.

Plato

"The two most important days in your life are the day you are born and the day you find out why."

Mark Twain

The mind is not a vessel that needs filling, but wood that needs igniting.

Plutarch

It is curious to reflect upon the remarkable legend of the **Philosopher's Stone,** one of the oldest and most universal beliefs, the origin of which, however far back we penetrate into the records of the past, we do not probably trace its real source.

Frederick Soddy

> Just because you're paranoid doesn't mean they aren't after you.
>
> Joseph Heller

We shall not cease from exploration and the end of all our exploring will be to arrive where we started and know the place for the first time.

T.S. Eliot

The greatest discovery of any generation is that a human can alter his life by altering his attitude.

William James

Until they become conscious they will never rebel, and until after they have rebelled they cannot become conscious.

George Orwell

He who controls the past controls the future. He who controls the present controls the past.

George Orwell

We are what we think, all that we are arises with our thoughts, with our thoughts we make the world.

Buddha

Nothing's gonna change my world
Nothing's gonna change my world
Nothing's gonna change my world
Nothing's gonna change my world

John Lennon

"I go to the *Upanishads* to ask questions."

Niels Bohr

"Where Jesus lives, the great-hearted gather. We are a door that is never locked. If you are suffering any kind of pain, stay near this door. Open it."

Rumi

Once upon a time, the gods gathered and decided to send yet another mission to Planet Earth. A briefing was held to prepare for the descent. Those that would go chose to become human and would have to lose all memory of their divinity. *Their task would be to discover one another on Earth, recover their memories through intuition, and piece together the members of the descent.* In the darkness that covered the earth, these individuals and sacred places were points of scattered light in a web which bound the dark: *a scattering of people, a light webby tension of them everywhere over the globe.*

Doris Lessing

An ordinary truth is a statement whose opposite is a falsehood. A profound truth is a statement whose opposite is also a profound truth.

Niels Bohr

Vocatus Atque Non,

Vocatus Deus Aderit.

Bidden or not bidden,

God is present.

"Why, sometimes I've believed as many as six impossible things before breakfast."

Lewis Carroll

You will always exist in the universe in one form or another.

Shunryu Suzuki

I would like to beg you, dear sir, to have patience with everything unresolved in your heart and to try to love the questions themselves as if they were locked rooms or books written in a very foreign language. Don't search for the answers, which could not be given to you now, because you would not be able to live them. And the point is, to live everything. Live the questions now. Perhaps then, some day in the far future, you will gradually, without even noticing it, live your way into the answer.

Rainer Maria Rilke

"What is your way?"

Daojian answered, "To be free wherever I am."

Zen Mondo

*The human heart can go to the lengths of God.
Dark and cold we may be, but this
Is no winter now. The frozen misery
Of centuries breaks, cracks, begins to move,
The thunder is the thunder of the floes, the thaw, the flood, the upstart Spring.
Thank God our time is now when wrong
Comes up to face us everywhere,
Never to leave us till we take
The longest stride of soul men ever took.
Affairs are now soul size
The enterprise
Is exploration into God.
Where are you making for? It takes
So many thousand years to wake,
But will you wake for pity's sake?*

Christopher Fry

The Soul is our True Self, though we may not be aware of its existence until the very moment of the body's death.

Elmer Green

Philosophy is man's expression of curiosity about everything and his attempt to make sense of the world primarily through his intellect.

Alan Watts

This is the real secret of life – to be completely engaged with what you are doing in the here and now. And instead of calling it work, realize it is play.

Alan Watts

Voici mon secret. Il est tres simple:

On ne voit bien qu'avec le coeur. L'essentiel est invisible pour les yeux.

Antoine de Saint-Exupery

The task is not so much to see what no one yet has seen, but to think what nobody yet has thought about that which everybody sees.

Arthur Schopenhauer

Nurture your mind with great thoughts, for you will never go any higher than you **think.**

Benjamin Disraeli

Do not dwell in the past, do not dream of the future, concentrate the mind on the present moment.

Buddha

Teaching without words and
work without doing
are understood by very few.

Lao Tzu

What will be, is.

Robert Graves

That that is is.

Shakespeare

As, after casting away worn
out garments,
A man later takes new ones,
So after casting away worn
out bodies,
The embodied Self
encounters other, new ones.

Bhagavad Gita

Empathy is the secret to most things in life ~ including magic.

Deborah Harkness

…you are indestructible, immortal. This is not a belief. It is absolute certainty that needs no external evidence or proof from some secondary source.

Eckhart Tolle

Only your sense "I am," though in the world, is not of the world.

Sri Nisargadatta Maharaj

Realization doesn't destroy the individual any more than the reflection of the moon breaks a drop of water. A drop of water can reflect the whole sky.

Dogen

There is only one time when it is essential to awaken.

That time is now.

The Buddha

They say that Paradise will be perfect...

We hold on to times like this then, since this is how it's going to be...

Rumi

Now and then it's good to pause in our pursuit of happiness and just **be happy.**

Guillaume Apollinaire

The invariable mark of wisdom is seeing the miraculous in the common.

Ralph Waldo Emerson

Everyday we should hear at least one little song, read one good poem, see one exquisite picture, and, if possible, speak a few sensible words.

Johann Wolfgang von Goethe

This is my simple religion.

There is no need for temples; no need for complicated philosophy.

Our own brain, our own heart is our temple;

the **philosophy** is kindness.

Dalai Lama

**People don't realize that now is all there ever is:
There is no past or future except as memory or anticipation in your mind.**

Eckhart Tolle

There are two lasting bequests we can hope to give our children. One of these is roots, the other, wings.

Johann Wolfgang von Goethe

What we have called matter is energy, whose vibration has been so lowered as to be perceptible to the senses.

There is no matter.

Albert Einstein

If you want to find the secrets of the universe, think in terms of energy, frequency and vibration.

Nikola Tesla

"It isn't necessary to get there, just get going."

Elmer Green

(Detach from Outcome)

"Think of something happy to shout as we go."

Rumi

You never know how strong you are, until being strong is your only choice.

Bob Marley

Never was there a time when I did
not exist, nor you, nor all the kings;
nor in the future
shall any of us cease to be.

Bhagavad-Gita

New beginnings are often disguised as painful endings.

Lao Tzu

"Death is just where your suit falls off and now you're in your other suit."

George Harrison

They say that I am dying, but I am not going away. Where could I go?

I am here...

Sri Ramana Maharshi

Even philosophers will praise war as ennobling mankind, forgetting the Greek who said:

"War is bad in that it begets more evil than it kills."

Immanuel Kant

The day science begins to study non-physical phenomena, it will make more progress in one decade than in all the previous centuries of its existence.

Nikola Tesla

If quantum mechanics hasn't profoundly shocked you, you haven't understood it yet.

Niels Bohr

In teaching you cannot see the fruit of a day's work. It is invisible and remains so, maybe for twenty years.

Jacques Barzun

If thou but settest foot on this Path, thou shalt see it everywhere.

Hermes Trismegistus

Look at every path closely and deliberately. Try it as many times as you think necessary. Then ask yourself and yourself alone one question...Does this path have a heart? If it does, it is good. If it doesn't, it is of no use.

Carlos Castaneda

To know how to choose a path with heart is to learn how to follow intuitive feeling. Logic can tell you superficially where a path might lead to, but it cannot judge whether your heart will be in it.

Jean Shinoda Bolen

The truth of course is that there is no journey. We are arriving and departing all at the same time.

David Bowie

There is always one moment in childhood when the door opens and lets the future in.

Graham Greene

The voyage of discovery is not in seeking new landscapes but in having new eyes.

Marcel Proust

...the universe is a single living creature that encompasses all living creatures within it.

Plato

"When it comes your time to die, be not like those whose hearts are filled with the fear of death, so that when their time comes they weep and pray for a little more time to live their lives over again in a different way. Sing your death song and die like a **hero** going home."

Chief Tecumsah

If myth is translated into literal fact, then myth is a lie. But if you read it as a reflection of the world inside you, then it's true. Myth is the penultimate truth.

Joseph Campbell

"As we live, we seem to move through a succession of NOWS, and the question is, what are they? We have the strong impression that things have definite positions relative to each other. I aim to abstract away everything we cannot see and simply keep this idea of many different things coexisting as one. There are simply the NOWS, nothing more, nothing less."

Julian Barbour

"It is change that provides the illusion of time."

Josh Richardson

We are here to awaken from the illusion of our separateness.

Thich Nhat Hanh

Who looks outside,
dreams;

Who looks inside,
awakes.

Carl Jung

You cannot be rid of problems without abandoning illusions.

Sri Nisargadatta Maharaj

True knowledge is not attained by thinking. It is what you are; it is what you become.

Sri Aurobindo

*Only the illimitable Permanent
is here.
A Peace stupendous, featureless, still
replaces all, -- what once was I, in it
A silent unnamed emptiness content
Either to fade in the Un-Knowable
Or thrill with luminous seas of the Infinite.*

                      Sri Aurobindo
                          Savitri

I ask you to believe nothing that you cannot verify for yourself.

G.I. Gurdjieff

To know means to know all.
Not to know all means not to know.
In order to know all, it is only necessary to know a little. But, in order to know this little it is first necessary to know pretty much.

G.I. Gurdjieff

I already knew then as an undoubted fact that beyond the thin film of false reality there existed another reality from which, for some reason, something separated us. The "miraculous" was a penetration into this unknown reality.

P.D. Ouspensky

The aim of art is to represent not the outward appearance of things, but their inward significance.

Aristotle

An optimist may see a light where there is none, but why must the pessimist always run to blow it out?

Rene Descartes

All men begin their learning with **Homer**.

Xenophanes

"Facts are meaningless. You could use facts to prove anything that's even remotely true."

Homer Simpson

The only true wisdom is in knowing you know nothing.

Socrates

The pessimist complains about the wind;

the optimist expects it to change;

the realist adjusts the sails.

> William Arthur Ward

Always be on the lookout for the presence of wonder.

E. B. White

There is nothing either good or bad but thinking makes it so.

William Shakespeare

Before death takes what you're given,

Give away what's there to give.

Rumi

I have realized that the past and future are real illusions; that they exist only in the present, which is what there is and all there is.

Alan Watts

Nature does not hurry, yet everything is accomplished.

Lao Tzu

There is only one corner of the universe you can be certain of improving, and that's your own self.

Aldous Huxley

Ceci n'est pas une pipe.

Rene Magritte

Each day of our lives we make deposits in the memory banks of our children.

Charles R. Swindoll

> Children are human beings to whom respect is due, superior to us by reason of their innocence and of the greater possibilities of their future.
>
> Maria Montessori

Have the courage to use your own reason – that is the motto of enlightenment.

Immanuel Kant

The entire universe is a great theatre of mirrors.

Alice Ann Bailey

We are not human doings!

We are human beings.

Chungliang Al Huang

The infinite vibratory levels, the dimensions of interconnectedness are without end. There is nothing independent. All beings and things are residents in your awareness.

Alex Grey

And, when you want something, all the universe conspires in helping you achieve it.

Paulo Coelho

Reprogramming the unconscious beliefs that block fuller awareness of creative intuitive capabilities depends upon a key characteristic of the mind, namely that it responds to what is vividly imagined as though it were real experience.

Willis Harman

You are not a human being in search of a spiritual experience. You are a spiritual being immersed in a human experience.

Pierre Teilhard de Chardin

Nothing is permanent in this world, not even our troubles.

Charlie Chaplin

Mystics understand the roots of the Tao but not its branches; scientists understand its branches but not its roots.

Science does not need mysticism and mysticism does not need science; but man needs both.

Fritjof Capra

What I thought was unreal now, for me, seems in some ways to be more real than what I think to be real, which seems now to be unreal.

Fred Alan Wolf

When you are free from delusion, you can enjoy illusion.

Enjoy the dream but enjoy the dream being free.

Mooji

There are more things in heaven and earth, Horatio,

Than are dreamt of in your philosophy.

William Shakespeare

This above all: to thine own self be true, and it must follow, as the night the day, thou canst not then be false to any man.

William Shakespeare

When one is without ego, one becomes immediately free of all personal judgments, and perceives life and the world with divine eyes and mind. Nothing is offensive to them and they remain in perfect serenity and peace always.

Mooji

The moment you realize you are not present, you are present.

Eckhart Tolle

Life isn't about finding yourself.

Life is about creating yourself.

George Bernard Shaw

We are what our thoughts have made us; so take care about what you think. Words are secondary.

Thoughts live; they travel far.

Swami Vivekananda

There will be no end to the troubles of states, or of humanity itself, till **philosophers** become kings in this world, or till those we now call kings and rulers really and truly become philosophers, and political power and philosophy thus come into the same hands.

Plato

If we do discover a complete theory, it should be in time understandable in broad principle by everyone. Then we shall all, philosophers, scientists and just ordinary people be able to take part in the discussion of why we and the universe exist.

Stephen Hawking

The worth of a civilization or a culture is not valued in the terms of its material wealth or military power, but by the quality and achievements of its representative individuals – its philosophers, its poets and its artists.

Herbert Read

Beliefs are where it's at, and if you believe, you can do anything. Believe in yourself, and only good things can happen.

Love, Ted

Ted Williams, Tuscarora Nation

> You ask a philosopher a question and after he or she has talked for a bit, you don't understand your question any more.
>
> Philippa Foot

Life in the past is a story to learn from, and the present is something to experience. It is all changeable, all myth, all celebration, all learning.

David Chethlahe Paladin

The true work of art is born from the "artist": a mysterious, enigmatic and mystical creation. It detaches itself from him, it acquires an autonomous life, becomes a personality, an independent subject, animated with a spiritual breath, the living subject of a real existence of being.

Wassily Kandinsky

When I look back at my life experiences, they are no more real to me than if they were in a storybook. Maybe that is the beauty of it.

David Chethlahe Paladin

And I'll rise up
I'll rise like the day
I'll rise up
I'll rise unafraid
I'll rise up
And I'll do it a thousand times again
And I'll rise up High like the waves
I'll rise up in spite of the ache
I'll rise up
And I'll do it a thousand times again
For you
For you
For you
For you

Andra Day

A growing and increasingly influential movement of **philosophers**, ethicists, law professors and activists are convinced that the great moral struggle of our time will be for the rights of animals.

Michael Pollan

It's always amazed me how little attention philosophers, psychologists or anyone else actually has paid to humor.

Edward de Bono

And if that wasn't funny, there were lots of things that weren't even funnier.

Joseph Heller

"I never met a man I didn't like until I met Will Rogers."

Mort Sahl

There is no great genius without a mixture of madness.

Aristotle

Do not dwell in the past, do not dream of the future, concentrate the mind on the present moment.

Buddha

If thou suffer injustice, console thyself; the true unhappiness is in doing it.

Democritus

The nature of God is a circle
of which the center is
everywhere and the
circumference is nowhere.

Empedocles

The essence of **philosophy** is that a man should so live that his happiness shall depend as little as possible on external things.

Epictetus

The senses deceive from time to time, and it is prudent never to trust wholly those who have deceived us even once.

Rene Descartes

Nothing is more active than thought , for it travels over the universe....
Thales

Of all the things which wisdom provides to make us entirely happy, much the greatest is the possession of friendship.

Epicurus

Laughter is a sunbeam of the soul.

Thomas Mann

Death is not an event in life: we do not live to experience death. If we take eternity to mean not infinite temporal duration but timelessness, then eternal life belongs to those who live in the present.

Ludwig Wittgenstein

If a lion could talk, we could not understand him.

Ludwig Wittgenstein

You are what you think.

All that you are arises from your thoughts. With your thoughts you make your world.

The Dhammpada

The mysterious power of thought enables it to produce external, perceptible, phenomenal results by its own inherent energy.

Helena Blavatsky

Their little universe is very young, and its god is still a child. But it is too soon to judge them; when We return in the Last Days, We will consider what should be saved.

Arthur C. Clarke

He had decided to live forever or die in the attempt.

Joseph Heller

Get over it, and accept the inarguable conclusion. The universe is immaterial -- mental and spiritual.

R.C. Henry

To truly know the world, look deeply within your own being;

to truly know yourself, take real interest in the world.

Rudolf Steiner

> In all the areas within which the spiritual life of humanity is at work, the historical epoch wherein fate has placed us is an epoch of stupendous happenings.

— Edmund Husserl

When I was a boy and I would see scary things in the news, my mother would say to me, "Look for the helpers. You will always find people who are helping."

Mr. Rogers

Your imaginings can have as much power over you as your reality, or even more.

Charles Tart

The body does not end with our skin – it extends into time, into space and into other people.

Stanley Krippner

Don't get addicted to being human.

This is only temporary.

Robert Monroe

I have absolutely no fear of death. From my near-death research and my personal experiences, death is, in my judgment, simply a transition into another kind of reality.

Raymond Moody

To know yourself as the Being underneath the **thinker**, the stillness underneath the mental noise, the love and joy underneath the pain, is **freedom, salvation, enlightenment.**

Eckhart Tolle

My thought is me:

that is why I cannot stop thinking. I exist because I think I cannot keep from thinking.

Jean-Paul Sartre

Only the guy who isn't rowing has time to rock the boat.

Jean-Paul Sartre

Live your life as though your every act were to become a universal law.

Immanuel Kant

All truth passes through three stages:

First, it is ridiculed.

Second, it is violently opposed.

Third, it is accepted as being self-evident.

Arthur Schopenhauer

Be kind, for everyone you meet is fighting a great battle.

Philo of Alexandria

There is nothing so absurd that some **philosopher** has not already said it.

Cicero

When I die I will soar with angels~

And when I die to the angels...

What I shall become,

You cannot imagine.

Rumi

The illegality of cannabis is outrageous, an impediment to full utilization of a drug which helps produce the serenity and insight, sensitivity and fellowship so desperately needed in this increasingly mad and dangerous world.

Carl Sagan

In the depth of winter
I finally learned that
there was in me an
invincible summer.

Albert Camus

There is always some madness in love. But there is also always some reason in madness.

Friedrich Nietzsche

From the idea that the self is not given to us, I think there is only one practical consequence:

We have to create ourselves as a work of art.

Michel Foucault

What a piece of work is a man, how noble in reason, how infinite in faculties in form and moving how express and admirable, in action how like an angel, in apprehension how like a god.

William Shakespeare

Life can only be understood backwards; but it must be lived forwards.

Soren Kierkegaard

What I call the human qualities are love, compassion, tolerance, will. To be *warm-hearted* – that is true human being.

You see, not to have warm feeling in the heart; that is almost not to have fully the nature of a human.

The Dalai Lama

My technique is don't believe in anything. If you believe in something you are precluded from believing in its opposite.

Terrence McKenna

All the earth is mine and I have a right to go all over it and through it.

Apollonius of Tyana

I had discovered, early in my researches, that the alchemists' doctrine was no mere chemical fantasy, but a **philosophy** they applied to the world, to the elements and to man himself.

William Butler Yeats

*If you are here unfaithfully with us,
you're causing terrible damage.
If you've opened your loving to God's love,
you're helping people you don't know and have never seen.*

*Is what I say true? Say yes quickly,
If you know,
if you've known it from before the beginning of the universe.*

Rumi

"You have to do everything you can, you have to work your hardest and if you stay positive you have a shot at a silver lining."

Silver Linings Playbook

"There ain't no answer. There ain't gonna be any answer. There never has been an answer. There's the answer."

Gertrude Stein

I think we all have a core that's ecstatic, that knows and that looks up in wonder. We all know that there are marvelous moments of eternity that just happen. We know them.

Coleman Barks

Eventually, child, you will come to the land of the dead with no effort, no risk, a safe, calm journey, in the company of your own death guide, your special, devoted friend, who's been beside you every moment of your life, who knows you better than yourself --

Philip Pullman

Resolve to be tender with the young,

compassionate with the aged,

sympathetic with the striving,

and tolerant with the weak and wrong.

Sometime in your life, you will have been all of these.

Buddha

A fundamental conclusion of the new physics acknowledges that the observer creates the reality.

R.C. Henry

Not only is the universe stranger than we think, it is stranger than we can think.

Werner Heisenberg

My mind was formed by studying philosophy...

Werner Heisenberg

...I'm looking for the face I had, before the world was made....

W.B. Yeats

"The more real you get, the more unreal the world gets..."

John Lennon

It isn't what we don't know that gives us trouble, it's what we know that ain't so.

Will Rogers

Music is a higher revelation than all wisdom and **philosophy.**

Ludwig von Beethoven

*Most people think,
Great God will come from the skies,
Take away everything
And make everybody feel high.
But if you know what life is worth,
You will look for yours on earth:
And now you see the light,
You stand up for your rights.
Jah!*

Bob Marley

Jah knows how I try

Stephen Marley

You are already that which you want to be, and your refusal to believe this is the only reason you do not see it.

Neville Goddard

Now never ends.

Schroedinger

The universe is a dream dreamed by a single dreamer where all the dream characters dream too.

Arthur Schopenhauer

Talent hits a target no one else an hit;

Genius hits a target no one else can see.

Arthur Schopenhauer

It is time for parents to teach young people early on that in diversity there is beauty and there is strength.

Maya Angelou

Up in the morning, up in the morning
Out on the job, well, you've got me searching for
Searching for, the philosophers stone...

Even my best friends
Even my best friends they don't know
That my job is turning lead into gold

When you hear that engine
When you hear that engine drone
I'm on the road again and I'm searching for
The Philosophers Stone

Van Morrison

I am in that state where there is total absence of any concept of presence or absence. You are also in that state but you don't know it.

Sri Nisargadatta Maharaj

Until one is committed there is hesitancy…whatever you can do or dream you can, begin it. Boldness has genius, power and magic in it.

Goethe

Alchemy is a kind of **philosophy:**

a kind of thinking that leads to a way of understanding.

Marcel Duchamp

"I know you're out there. I can feel you now. I know that you're afraid...you're afraid of us. You're afraid of change. I don't know the future. I didn't come here to tell you how this is going to end. I came here to tell you how it's going to begin. I'm going to hang up this phone, and then I'm going to show these people what you don't want them to see. I'm going to show them a world without you. A world without rules and controls, without borders or boundaries. A world where anything is possible. Where we go from there is a choice I leave to you."

Neo

"At the end of *MATRIX* Neo tells MATRIX that now that a human has established mastery over it, the entire human race is freed. That hopeful line, however, is incorrect. Life isn't that simple.

We are all Neos, and each of us must take responsibilities for our own salvation.

…until we "wake up" and become conscious, we are in large parts puppets of unconscious processes, denial by the ego notwithstanding. The Wachowski Brothers understood this."

Elmer Green

The matrix is everywhere. It is all around us. Even now, in this very room.

You can see it when you look out your window or when you turn on your television. You can feel it when you go to work, when you go to church, when you pay your taxes. It is the world that has been pulled over your eyes, to blind you from the truth.

We are living in a dream world within a dream world – a Matrix within the virtual-reality universe – and it is being broadcast from the Moon.

Morpheus

"I would like to see every single soldier on every single side, just take off your helmet, unbuckle your kit, lay down your rifle, and set down at the side of some shady lane, and say, nope, I ain't a gonna kill nobody. Plenty of rich folks wants to fight.
Give them the guns."

Woody Guthrie

As the soul leaves its body, it remains enveloped with the quality of Light that it acquired through the choices that it made while it was upon the Earth.

Gary Zukav

The world, like a stream full of attachment and aversions seems real until the *awakening.*

Shankara

Holden:

"Don't ever tell anybody anything.
If you do you start missing everybody."

J.D. Salinger

The final answer is this:

Nothing is.

Sri Nisargadatta Maharaj

The basic difference between an ordinary person and a warrior is that a warrior takes everything as a challenge while an ordinary person takes everything either as a blessing or a curse.

Carlos Castaneda

What lies before us and what lies behind us are small matters compared to what lies within us. And when you bring what is within out into the world, miracles happen.

Thoreau

All are lunatics, but he who can analyze his delusions is called a **philosopher**.

Ambrose Bierce

To have no time for philosophy is to be a true philosopher.

Pascal

Stop thinking, and end your problems.

Lao Tzu

Whatever you think about with desire or fear appears before you as real.

Sri Nisargadatta Maharaj

As the same person inhabits the body through childhood, youth and old age; so too at the time of death, he attains another body. The wise are not deluded by these changes.

Bhagavad Gita

"I'm an *American,*

I don't believe in *'philosophy'.*"

Ted 2

A bottle of wine contains more philosophy than all the books in the world.

Louis Pasteur

.
.
.
.
.
.
.
.

The bad news is you're falling through the air, nothing to hang on to, no parachute. The good news is there's no ground.

Chogyam Trungpa

The primary cause of unhappiness is never the situation but your thoughts about it."

Eckhart Tolle

Meet everybody and every circumstance on the battlefield of life with the courage of a hero and the smile of a conqueror.

Paramhansa Yogananda

After silence, that which comes nearest to expressing the inexpressible is music.

Aldous Huxley

I'm not telling you it's going to be easy.
I'm telling you it's going to be worth it.

Art Williams

The way we talk to children becomes their inner voice.

Peggy O'Mara

The supreme prerogative of childhood is wonder...Is it any wonder that so many of the great geniuses and innovators are those who have kept their childhood alive in them. **Wonder** has a buoyant, exhilarating crest-of-the-wave effect.

Jean Houston

"It is through fantasy that children achieve catharsis. It is the best means they have for taming
wild things."

Maurice Sendak

What a liberation to realize that the *"voice in my head"* is not who I am. Who am I then? The one who sees that.

Eckhart Tolle

Enlightenment is the ego's ultimate disappointment.

Chogyam Trungpa

There are no others.
Sri Ramana Maharshi

I lived on the shady side of the road and watched my neighbor's gardens across the way reveling in the sunshine.
I felt I was poor, and from door to door went with my hunger.
The more they gave me from their careless abundance the more I became aware of my beggar's bowl.
Till one morning I awoke from my sleep at the sudden opening of my door, and you came and asked for alms.
In despair I broke the lid of my chest open and was startled into finding my own wealth.

Rabindranath Tagore

In the olden days, I believe Mozart also improvised on piano, but somehow in the last 200 years, the whole training of Western classical music – they don't read between the lines, they just read the lines.

Ravi Shankar

Only the impossible is worth doing.

Choje Akong Tolku Rinpoche

One good deed is worth a thousand prayers.

Zarathustra

The eye with which I see God is the same eye with which God sees me.

Meister Eckhart

Your body is merely a machine made to express the thoughts that flow through you and nothing more. It is but an instrument for you to express your imagings just as a piano is an instrument for a musician to express his imagings. Just as the piano is not the musician, so, likewise, your body is not you.

Walter Russell

The soul is immortal.

Socrates

There exists only the present instant...a Now which always and without end is itself new.

There is no yesterday nor any tomorrow, but only Now, as it was a thousand years ago and as it will be a thousand years hence.

Meister Eckhart

When you change the way you look at things, the things you look at change.

Max Planck

When I look inside and see that I am nothing, that's wisdom.

When I look outside and see that I am everything, that's love...

between these two my life turns.

Sri Nisargadatta

When you rise in the morning, give thanks for the light, for your life, for your strength.

Give thanks for your food and for the joy of living.

Tecumseh

Silence is one of the great arts of conversation.

Cicero

Each morning, we are born again.

What we do today is what matters most.

Buddha

To be wronged is nothing unless you continue to remember it.

Confucius

Whatever you can do or dream you can, begin it.

Boldness has genius, power and magic in it.

Begin it now.

Goethe

The reading of all good books is like a conversation with the finest minds of past centuries.

Descartes

Knowing yourself is the beginning of all wisdom.

Aristotle

Those who know do not speak.

Those who speak do not know.

Lao Tzu

It's not what happens to you,
but how you react to it that
matters.

Epictetus

Fear not the strangeness you feel. The future must enter you long before it happens.

Just wait for the birth, for the hour of new clarity.

Rainer Maria Rilke

"I don't pretend to have all the answers. I don't pretend to even know what the questions are. Hey, where am I?"

Jack Handey

What you call real – all the good and ill of human life – is illusion.

Carl Jung

Wake up before death comes and surprises you. One day the body will drop away. In this world, everything that comes also goes. But the Self does not die. The inner Self is ageless and unchanging. Death cannot reach it.

Swami Muktananda

Light and darkness, these paths are thought to be the world's everlasting paths. By the one, one goes not to return; by the other, one returns again.

The Upanishads

Philosophy must find its justification in daily existence; otherwise it remains only a theory among other theories, instead of an essential quest by which each of us, in a vision of love, collaborates with the great work of nature.

Frederic Lionel

Beauty is eternity gazing at itself in a mirror.

But you are eternity and you are the mirror.

Kahlil Gibran

The Truth is not an experience or an idea.

The Truth is that you have been dreaming.

Wake Up!

Adyashanti

When thought enters into the changeless it goes silent. When thought goes silent: the *thinker*, the psychological me, the image-produced self, disappears. Suddenly it is gone. You, as an idea, are gone.
Awareness remains alone.

If you want to wake up, the first thing you need to seriously consider is that you are asleep and everything you take as real is a dream.

Adyashanti

Poetry is the lifeblood of rebellion, revolution and the raising of consciousness.

Alice Walker

I think that the task of **philosophy** is not to provide answers, but to show how the way we perceive a problem can be itself part of a problem.

Slavoj Zizek

Which do you think is larger, the highest mountain on earth or the pile of bones that represents the lives that you have lived over and over in every realm governed by the patterns of your own karma? Greater, my friends, is the pile of bones than the highest mountain on earth.

The Buddha

If you are depressed, you are living in the past.

If you are anxious, you are living in the future.

If you are at peace, you are living in the present.

Lao Tzu

Empathy is the ability to imagine yourself in someone else's position and to intuit what that person is feeling. It is the ability to stand in others' shoes, to see with their eyes, and to feel with their hearts... *Empathy* makes us human. *Empathy* brings joy. And, empathy is an essential part of living a life of meaning.

Daniel H. Pink

Everything you can imagine is real.

Picasso

*I, too, sing America.
I am the darker brother.
They send me to eat in the kitchen
When company comes,
But I laugh,
And eat well,
And grow strong.*

*Tomorrow,
I'll be at the table
When company comes.
Nobody'll dare
Say to me,
"Eat in the kitchen,"
Then.*

*Besides,
They'll see how beautiful I am
And be ashamed.
I, too, am America.*

Langston Hughes

Art requires **philosophy**, just as philosophy requires art. Otherwise, what would become of beauty?

Paul Gauguin

Time is what prevents everything from happening at once.

John Archibald Wheeler

Think for yourself and question authority.

Timothy Leary

I am getting so far out one day I won't come back at all.

William S. Burroughs

You're only as young as the last time you changed your mind.

Timothy Leary

"Sometimes paranoia's just having all the facts."

William S. Burroughs

The man who realizes his ignorance has taken the first step toward **knowledge.**

Mac Heindel

One cannot attain enlightenment only by understanding the Buddha's teachings in one's mind; great compassion is essential.

Chatral Sangye Dorje Rinpoche

"Everyone wants a magical solution to their problem, and everyone refuses to believe in magic."

The Mad Hatter

The most important thing is that we are living in the most important time in the history of the universe…there are thousands of souls who want to be here to experience this – even if they can just be here for a few hours…They can say "I was there when this occurred." This is how important this is to the entire universe…We're moving away from the negativity of the Old Earth.

Dolores Cannon

Do not seek to follow in the footsteps of the wise. Seek what they sought.

Matsuo Basho

What you are today is the choice you made yesterday.

Tsem Tulku Rinpoche

"I saw the angel in the marble and carved until I set him free."

Michelangelo

If you are lonely when you're alone, you are in bad company.

Sartre

"It's a sad man, my friend, who's livin' in his own skin and can't stand the company."

Springsteen

Everything is energy and that's all there is to it. Match the frequency of the reality you want and you cannot help but get that reality. It can be no other way. This is not **philosophy**. This is physics.

Einstein

Think about the game.

Damn Yankees

I don't think there is any **truth**. There are only points of view.
Whoever controls the media, the images, controls the culture.

Allen Ginsberg

Death is only an experience through which you are meant to learn a great lesson:

you cannot die.

Paramahansa Yogananda

The treasure that is precious is **even-mindedness** in all situations.

Sai Baba

A mind *stretched*
by a **new idea**
can never **go back**
to its original
dimensions

Oliver Wendell Holmes

After you die, you wear what you are.

St. Teresa of Avila

Do not go where the path may lead; go instead where there is no path and leave a trail.

Ralph Waldo Emerson

The miracle is not to walk on water; the miracle is to walk on the green earth, dwelling deeply in the present moment and feeling truly alive.

Thich Nhat Hanh

The theorems of **philosophy** are to be enjoyed as much as possible, as if they were ambrosia and nectar; for the pleasure arising from them is genuine, incorruptible and divine.

Pythagoras

There is a time when the unknown reveals itself in a mysterious way to the spirit of man. A sudden rent in the veil of darkness will make manifest things hitherto unseen
and then close again upon the
mysteries within.

Victor Hugo

Very little is needed to make a happy life; it is all within yourself, in your way of thinking.

Marcus Aurelius

*"Sometimes I sits and I thinks.
And sometimes I just sits."*

Tigger

It is impossible to begin to learn that which one thinks one already knows.

Epictetus

> The past is never dead,
> It is not even past.
>
> William Faulkner

Be content with what you have; rejoice in the way things are. When you realize there is nothing lacking, the whole world belongs to you.

Lao Tzu

Once you make a decision, the universe conspires to make it happen.

Ralph Waldo Emerson

Love should be like breathing. It should be just a quality in you – wherever you are, with whoever you are, or even if you are alone, love goes on overflowing from you. It is not a question of being in love with someone – it is a question of being love.

Osho

Your perspective is always limited by how much you know. Expand your knowledge and you will transform your mind.

Dr. Bruce Lipton

The first gulp from the glass of natural sciences will make you an atheist, but at the bottom of the glass God is waiting for you.

Werner Heisenberg

The Great spiritual geniuses, whether it was Moses, Buddha, Plato, Socrates, Jesus or Emerson...have taught man to look within himself to find God.

Ernest Holmes

Zen is liberation from time.
For if we open our eyes and
see clearly, it becomes
obvious that there is no other
time than this instant,
and that the past and the
future are abstractions
without any concrete reality.

Alan Watts

Sometimes people don't want to hear the truth because they don't want their illusions destroyed.

Friedrich Nietzsche

NOSCI TE IPSUM

Know thyself.

There is a fifth dimension, beyond that which is known to man. It is a dimension as vast as space and as timeless as infinity. It is the middle ground between light and shadow, between science and superstition.

Rod Serling

Our love is our life itself. What our love is like determines how we live and therefore everything about what we are as human beings.

Emanuel Swedenborg

Everything in this world has a hidden meaning.

Nikos Kazantzakis

*The day of my birth, my death
began its walk.
It is walking toward me,
without hurrying.*

Jean Cocteau

Day after day we must seek the **Philosophers Stone,** and the Tao reminds us that our body serves as a cup in which to distill, drop by drop, our own immortality...

Frederic Lionel

What if I told you...that you are made up of an unbounded conscious and intelligent life energy that can never be created or destroyed. You are an eternal and vibrational non-local field of Awareness, forever connected to Source Energy ; curiously experiencing life in a mortal body but for a short time.

Morpheus

Relax. Nothing is under control.

Adi Da

"Oh, what'll you do now, my blue-eyed son? Oh, what'll you do now, my darling young one? I'm a-goin' back out 'fore the rain starts a-fallin', I'll walk to the depths of the deepest black forest, Where the people are many and their hands are all empty, Where the pellets of poison are flooding their waters, Where the home in the valley meets the damp dirty prison, Where the executioner's face is always well hidden, Where hunger is ugly, where souls are forgotten, Where black is the color, where none is the number, And I'll tell it and think it and speak it and breathe it, And reflect it from the mountain so all souls can see it, Then I'll stand on the ocean until I start sinkin', But I'll know my song well before I start singin', And it's a hard, it's a hard, it's a hard, it's a hard, It's a hard rain's a-gonna fall."

Bob Dylan

The softest thing in the universe overcomes the hardest thing in the universe.
That without substance can enter where there is no room.
Hence I know the value of non-action.

Teaching without words and work without doing
Are understood by very few.

Lao Tzu

We have not even to risk the
adventure alone,
for the heroes of all time have
gone before us.

Joseph Campbell

Mankind will cross the threshold into the spiritual world at the end of the century.

Rudolf Steiner

Stand at your threshold point, create your own reality there and decide your path. The whole of humanity stands beside you facing timelessness. Have compassion for those who have not yet woken.

Stanley Messenger

The future enters into us, in order to transform itself in us, long before it happens.

Rilke

Live as though the day were here.

Nietzsche

When you experience your wisdom and the power of things as they are, together as one, then you have access to tremendous vision and power in the world. You find that you are inherently connected to your own being. That is discovering **magic**.

Chogyam Trungpa

I believe that legends and myths are largely made of truth.

J.R.R. Tolkien

*We shall not cease from exploration
And the end of all our exploring
Will be to arrive where we started
And know the place for the first time.*

T. S. Eliot

If the only prayer you say
in your entire life is
"Thank-you" ~
that would suffice.

Meister Eckhart

Live life as though you might die tomorrow. Do what you would like to be doing, and do your best each day.

Bear Heart

Not only is the universe stranger than we think, it is stranger than we can think.

Werner Heisenberg

There you go, man, keep as cool as you can. Face piles of trials with smiles.

It riles them to believe that you perceive the web they weave.
Keep on thinking free.

The Moody Blues

ESTO EXCELLENS INTER SE

Be Excellent to Each Other

What we call the beginning is often the end. And to make an end is to make a beginning. The end is where we start from.

T.S. Eliot

No matter how hard the past you can always begin again.

Buddha

www.ingramcontent.com/pod-product-compliance
Lightning Source LLC
Chambersburg PA
CBHW051645040426
42446CB00009B/987